The Long-Lasting Grief of Foxes

The Long-Lasting Grief of Foxes

Chim Sher Ting

An Imprint of Mouthfeel Press

The Long-Lasting Grief of Foxes

Mouthfeel Press is an indie press publishing works in English and Spanish by new and established poets. We publish poetry, fiction, and non-fiction. Our print books are available through independent bookstores and online booksellers, or at author's readings.

Clash! is an imprint of Mouthfeel Press

Cover Art by Octavio Quintanilla
Art Title: Los días oscuros 253
Cover Design: Karen Dreher

Contact Information:

Mouthfeelbooks.com
Info.mouthfeelbooks@gmail.com

Print ISBN: 978-1-957840-22-2
Ebook ISBN: 978-1-957840-24-6

Published in the United States, 2023
First Printing in English
$12

Table of Contents

To my family, whose dragons haunt even our closest memories.

The Long-Lasting Grief of Foxes

Beyond the Lake

池塘里水满了，
雨也停了

Outside the attap hut, the rain spills like tea over the
mouth of a cup. First, a light trickle over the lip of the
lake, then a relentless outpouring through the kintsugi
fissures in its sides.

田边的稀泥里
到处是泥鳅

The earthworms accosted the mud, dragging their lyre-
limp bodies across the denuded soil, listening to the
world changing above them.

天天我等着你，
等着你捉泥鳅

Every day, I would follow my brother out into the fields,
watching our breaths rise against the slate-grey
convexity of the sky, the pebble clouds and roiling waves
of wind, turning topsoil over with our bare hands to build
mud castles from the waste of the land.

大哥哥，好不好?
等着你捉泥鳅

We'd plunge our hands deep into the gnarled limbs of
trees and catch appleseed from the ribs of their bark, turn
our faces to the clouds, jaws agape, and catch a string of
pearls between our teeth. The rain would fall like the
tears of a widow who knew far too much then nothing at
all — nothing mattered then.

天天我等着你，
等着你捉泥鳅

When my brother passed, we moved into the mahogany-walled apartments that reached so high, I believed they were Man's attempt to be one with the sky. We stopped running into the rain, choosing instead to draw the curtains — the world knew too much then frighteningly little.

大哥哥 ， 好不好?
咱们去捉泥鳅

They told me it'll get better and sometimes, I don't know which tragedy they are referring to. Sometimes, watching the clothes dry in the fish-bowl eye of the washing machine, I can almost believe their lie. So then, why do I feel so sad, like a girl wanting to move on when all the world has done is end?

藕断丝连[1]

O love,

What do you know
about sacrifice,

when your skin
is lighter than the sky?

What do you know
about holding a rabbit

and shooting it
between the eyes?

Of culling an accent and
skinning it to its core?

After the war, my grandfather still
dreams of the mountains from his childhood,

the red cormorant soaring with an
olive branch within its beak.

In every story,
someone berates Chang Er

for drinking the potion
and ascending to the moon.

But the last time someone
shortened her name to Chang,

---

[1] ŏu duàn sī lián: Even when the lotus root breaks, the fibres still remain.

she thought about the moon—how it made
even half an existence look beautiful.

Somewhere in the past, someone said
唱首儿歌[2] and thought of her.

Why is it when the houses have
collapsed all around us,

we always remember most
of the song from our childhood?

O love,
tell me how much it hurts

to be the boy with a bone in your throat
then multiply it by an existence.

In the 70s, we slow danced with
feather boas and washed-out cheong sams.

In the 80s, they announced they were closing
the Getai, cleaning up the streets.

We were always walking
backwards into an ending.

All around us,
the mountains,

their aching.

their haunting, damning
mountain sound.

---

[2] Chàng shǒu ér gē: Sing a children's song.

追求梦想[3]

I always wondered why 求? What makes of one to beg
for her dream? But Love is a train that never leaves the
station. The turning of wheels, the easy gush of tires
back-rolling on the asphalt. When the carriage is room
enough for us, and the chandeliers aren't hanging off
their limbs, and I am not drifting, circling the rims of the
glasses when I'm expired and contemplating the futility
of being a frog at the bottom of the well, it seems almost
liveable.

井底之蛙[4]

The frog sees only the sky and longs for it, not realising,
on the other face of the wall, there is a river that leads
into another ending. How, small as a rosary bead, it finds
its way through redwood and biloba to carve an eye out
the other side. Yet, where the river opens into the sea, I
can only imagine the shifting cloisonné patterns of each
dinner conversation. Every *I'm glad you're following
your dream,* but then *oh, how could you ever think to
leave?*

I know now why they call it 孝顺, or to flow with
the wishes of your elders. Every travel advertisement
neglects to mention the family. And every family holds
a candle, mouthful of ashes, at the wake of the leaving,
chanting *remember us, remember us.*

Come back.

---

[3] Zhuī qiú mèng xiǎng: Chasing the dream.
[4] Jǐng dǐ zhī wā: A frog at the bottom of the well, also used to describe a person of limited perspective.

5

And so, every meander of the river opens into another
ending, into another station that flashes under the same
umbrella sky, leading right back into the same backyard.

From the bottom of the well, love hangs like an amber
light that never changes, singing—love conquers all and,
sometimes, it is all we can convince ourselves is enough.

City of Lions

A bag of ice to the jaw because that September was a
broken clock and every train that rattled past the metal
shack was an escape plan rewritten

but I made it anyway—

I was every haunting melody sung through the morning
fog when they took a bullet to the skull, then *oh I didn't
mean to hurt you there,*

because somewhere, someone got rip-roaring drunk and
forgot the hills were burning.

If 旧 rhymes with 酒, do we only talk about the past
through a pint of pina colada?

Someone will say I'm not Chinese enough for not
drinking plum wine.

Someone will say I'm not Chinese for knowing how to
wield double negatives in a sentence.

I ate at the beef noodle store every night because I loved
the underdog, till they told me there wasn't space enough
for me.

When they told me I wrote my name wrong the first time
I signed off on the book, I didn't —

I wrote rain into a language that felt like riotfire.

Someone says maybe you should stop writing about pain, but knives don't blunt once I've stopped wielding them.

The words that sound like poetry in Chinese only ever speak about distance: 东海，岁月，银河.

And maybe I haven't found enough words that speak about the complexity of proximity — the soil that follows you

10 steps, 20 steps, into the next gas station when you're sure you've gotten away,

when every phoneme still feels like a living thing s/mothered.

Maybe the museum is you and how you've turned a mother tongue into a flood.

Maybe the punchline is you and how you've mispronounced your name into a curse.

The water under the bridge is still a mirror for those who've pried open a face into the abyss.

When you say 奇迹, it's like you're shouting "起(rise)!" into darkness.

When we've run far enough, like the river, we reach the end of one timeline and enter another body.

If I cast aside this tongue, what little remains?

If I cast aside this skin, what love am I worthy to keep?

In every timeline,
the body is a white lie, looking

out the rehab window
behind Maccas,

learning the golden arches
of its undoing,

waiting for absolution.

The Dragon Lady

You are a train going for miles
without applause. And then,
blue lights ringed by another version
of Harlem nights, the one
where you can be forgiven
for killing your past life
at the back of an antique car.
Because every dragon lady
holds her myth like a knife.
And the director yells, "Do it again!"
this act of unloving,
cascading down the aisle
to your foreign lover
while the car is swimming
through monochrome and white-
washed soundscapes. I think mostly
you're asking to be forgiven
for pulling up the temples with tape.
What do we make of acts of desperation?
The accent perjurious as a dream.
You said you never thought yourself
a sword wielder but for them,
you could've been anything.
When you look in the mirror,
do you remember where the light ends
and shadows begin?
Actually, moon-rabbit,
you said there could be another ending
        and we thought it'd be one
                that didn't involve a trainwreck
                going up in flames.

The train has been going for miles
beneath the white of the moon,
    and yellow is the saddest colour,
        the only one
        who has ever loved a thing.

On the Black-and-White Television, Our Lies Look a Little Less White

This is how a white lie begins:
    Through a back-lit alley,
damp with cigarette smoke and emerald rain,
    a single streetlamp skimming the length
        of a translucent red curtain.

The leading lady comes running
        down the streets, take 32,
    drenched in longing.
        Beautiful creature, the director says,
    if only she'd make herself a little more white.

When someone says token, I imagine
        the small quarter you push into
    the black-and-white television
        in the mama shop behind school.

The silver spit.
        The static brow.
    The slow stutter of an inheritance
        coming to life.

The ancestors from my grandfather's dream tell him
        there is a place for us here.

That the only difference between
        a lie and a dream is our disbelief.

But my friend tells me
        he watched Ip Man last weekend
and now he loves Kung Fu.

But my brother watches every
      re-run of The Green Hornet and says he wants
          to be the superhero, not the
     lame-ass Asian sidekick.

In every version, I have
      never seen a superhero I could love.

At the front of the beauty salon, 2:30 pm,
      hands coated in varnish and sodium glycolate,
         I don't talk about Shang-Chi. How he
    kung fus from a white man's fantasy.

After all, what saving could come from
      those who needed to be saved?

Brane Theory

In Chinese, we don't say contentment.

We say 知足:
To know when things are enough.

To see every ending and
still choose the same.

The rabbit from my childhood sits in
its cage, calculating every possibility.

My grandfather crop circles his childhood
dreams through the driver seat of a cab.

My grandma lets the white lady intercept
her path on the plane and apologises for existing.

When someone hypothesises where I'm from,
I say China though my distance

from that country and this is uniform.

This is the land of the free —
but what of freedom?

The mud skippers back home
circle the lake, then up the mangrove trees.

Here, the currents push back into history.

Everything you wish it could be
is on the other side of everything that is.

The white man says something in
manglish, and everyone laughs:

The self-inflating Kung Fu joke
and the isolation I can't comprehend.

In a universe borne of heated exchange,
he says humour is only relative.

We say 饮水思源[5] but half the
origin stories are a villain growing into its skin.

I've learnt the natural order of things:

The infinite universe
and the finite probability of victimhood.

In the legends,
the rabbit seals its lips,

Forces itself into the cauldron
as fodder for the lone huntsman.

The people applaud through
the bones of the cypress.

For the uncoupling of a body,
who has collided with the wolves,

And made peace
with the fire.

---

[5] We should be thankful how far we've come.

The Phoenix was a Dragon Who Never Mastered Love

O princess of misguided malcontent. Under their faces, thick and weighted like the Analects, how you ploughed through garden light and threadbare futon to birth a phoenix. Red-combed, speckle-tailed. Iridescent like a flare. They called it 怀孕 — this pregnancy enveloping the last clarion of good fortune. The flood before the judgment. The punishment before the storm. The laurels bursting like a severed bloodline.

As it grows, the Phoenix carries the day on its back like a broken animal. Even in winter, its stalk of feathers still sings of new beginnings—the hope for a world changing on the hinge of an ancestral wound. Yet, change, like the sunrise, comes slow. All bones and heat, flicker and fade. Like the family name we have surrendered to the nascent dragon. The dragon rises sometime later and catches the Phoenix blazing in its jaws.

By fire, what legends have been killed or born?

Even an animal of light knows its shadows the minute it is born.

后悔[6]:

Maybe we'll walk backwards through
                 the crystal archway, the jade
      heirloom, the yellow-wood shutters,
          the gentled curse hammered into the lime-
stone pillars, the burning hills, red smoke
             beneath your jaw, the vermilion birds,
     their portrait in the clerestory windows,
           the wooden sugarcane cart, their dreams
of inheritance and dowry of thorns, ingots
     shucked from blood clams and ginger
        water, lake-creased thumbs making water
           lilies from a mirage.

Backwards through the pale end
         of a sentence, the moon-knife of a
    period, through a garden of
           flooded light, eye of a tiger
     through a ripened belly, jewelweed,

Through the white broth of thighs,
         the oak-red blood-spill, the wilted
   stalk of breath, hands over
           the stomach, gutted blue, pulling
      at the thread of dawn, mouth
   puckered then shut forever, given
       to what giving
         has been necessary to exist.

---

[6] Meaning "to regret" also phoneticised similar to 回, meaning "to return".

Through what dynasty we have
          shamed to arrive at offspring
                number four, with
          wet skirts and softened thighs;
                What sin we have committed
in our past lives to birth another like ourselves.

What Is 家[7] but a Roof over a Withered Body?

Two strangers once met in a tearoom.

With a slip of paper that bleeds
like a foreign tongue,

a bond that binds
like the arms of a lotus.

They call it 嫁[8]
because this is a woman's home.

How we started at an ending:

The woman made small enough
to be invisible, feet bound with worm-rot,
hands bent like the tail of a wish-bone.

The mother-in-law that hangs
her husband's trousers from the ceiling, asking
her to walk beneath them

There was an exchange of hands, then
snake broth that tasted like wine, wine
that tasted like water.

Someone conjured the ancient mountains,
the bearded man and his outdated legacy.

---

[7] Chinese character for "Home"
[8] Chinese character for "Marriage"–made from a combination of the characters for "Woman" and "Home".

Tell me why, in the legends, the woman
is either the fox or the homewrecker.

When they first met, the man touched
an egg to the welt on her lips,

He said it was full and enough.

Her female ancestors will bear
willful witnesses to the truth,

The bruises stretched thin
on their shins, telling her

It gets better,
you will learn to love as we did.

And I want to walk back into
that tearoom that bright August day

When the snow was just
starting to fall, shouting,

Ma, don't do it.

Don't do it.

But I don't.

When the ending has found itself
full-circle,

what were we,
but women living

our mothers' lie?

Casual Chinese (n.):

In the 20s,
> Ma watches all the Cecilia Cheung movies on
> repeat. CeCe. She says, I'll give you an English
> name a white lover can pronounce. People only
> love the things they can name. And they will call
> you honey, sweetie, baby, because people only
> name the things they own. I still can't pronounce
> curcumin, mala the way she'd like me to. I still
> write to her from across the 7 sea-seas, from
> countries she cannot name. And once, in the dark
> of the kitchen, I saw them then — the curcumin
> and mala pulsing beneath the skin of my wrist
> under the sapphire blue back-light and I
> whispered, see,

I'm still half of every-

thing you've been wishing I could be.

That Language You're Trying to Learn When You are Sixty and Sitting at the Table with Your New-Found Friends Wondering when You Stopped Trying to Ask for Sauce

But you were a 回忆. Intention. And also, 意 meaning.
      Because how often have we dis-
    articulated what we intended?
The way we've phoneticised
      from zygomatic arch,
          maxillary and tongue.
  The breath pining for another pocket
             of space.
To try again. To hear
      your incisors tear through another root
  like a broken canal.
The myth is the phone that rings as fast
         as the person that wishes it.
    The cow that returns
      to the field that has been stripped.
I think we have learnt to separate
      the bird from the stone,
    the cord from its flowering stem.
The moon licks the wounds off
      the alphabet cards by an abandoned sewing kit.
The television sings of the local news broadcast
        like it is the latest Chinese opera.
Some day, your daughter will learn to pronounce
      "etymology" faster than you can.
Then she'll learn to pronounce "happiness" and wonder
  why that didn't come first.

"Etymology"[9]—because a word remains
truest to its meaning when unspoken,
and on *logia*, is split
            by syllable, pathos and teeth.
I think of dust that circles
      the aerial beams, sun-spokes and cable lines
only to land in another space.
Sand that softens into another shape
            once the horse has galloped its parts.
Nothing is as prone to misconception
            as black holes[10] and a throat.
To swim and come up with nothing but air.
月爱。水牛。夜流。
            Have you submerged of yourself so far
till you've seen the stars?
Where in an orbit of pressurised breaths,
      stutter of fragmented mandible, they drift
            horizontal like a bridge of magpies
To the place where you have been known.
When you could have said
      all you have been dying to mean.

---

[9] etymon meaning "true meaning" and -logia meaning "study or speaking of"

[10] A black hole, upon coming close to another star, throws it off its course and sets it on a different path.

Object Impermanence

Everything is a lesson in impermanence:
                Two yolks merging into a scallion sun,
        bouquets of bok choy peeling beneath the sink.

4000 years ago, Li Bai wrote a letter home,
                found that ink takes two days
        to fade into a watermark. Even less
                to disappear without a scar.

You said it's been a while since
                we've been to Yum Cha,
                and the shop around the corner has closed.
        (But I've never liked the shop anyway.)

You've told me you've forgotten how to say
                the word that sounds a lot like like but not
        so much like love.
                (And it's okay, we don't use it much anyway.)

But in all honesty, I never figured out
        the word you were referring to.

Like the game of broken telephone
                we played when I was child, I never
        understood what you meant to say:

The hunger that never seemed
                to be about food.

The bones riddled with exhaustion when
                sleep was never enough.

I tell you about
        all the awards I've won.

And you tell me,
      "You know, 大姨,
        she's moving to Sydney."
                   "Sydney"
"是的，你—"

               "Ma, 大姨 has been gone
               for the last 10 years"
Sometimes, on the phone,
       2000 miles apart, I can almost believe
    the people we're pretending to be.

The girl who reclaimed her miracle.
              The mother who's proof
    a miracle wouldn't last.

You tell me you're okay,
     but you still listen to 康定情歌
   and talk about running with the horses,
        occasionally conjure a family from ghosts.

And I realise, through
        the rattle of the breeze,
              the sodium lights,

   My body fleshed, a lonely island, in
           my mother's skin,

     Maybe none of us ever are.

Bak Kut Teh

肉:

You peel the chilli, layer by layer, unearthing a clot of
seeds from its copper pith. The soup simmers on the
stove, frothing sunset gold over the blue-gas flames,
drowned out by radio talk of the day's weather.

How's your day at school?

The meat melts off the bones in the pressure cooker,
pork fat dripping from softened limbs like snow from
black root on a winter morning.

It's fine.

You sift the remaining bone-stock with a colander,
flushed with thyme and aniseed. You tell me to scrape
the flesh off the bones with a knife and laugh when my
fingers slip, wrangling silver against each cord-like
sinew.

*Honey, there's more than one way
to get to the heart of things,*

You whisper as you pull out a larger knife and, taking
the pig trotter from my hands, whistle each hardened
tendon—splitting the ropes—off of the skeleton flower.

骨:

Some nights, snow swathes the streets in silent, sleet-wet
pavements. You call me on the phone while you're

peeling an orange, and like muscle memory, I say I'm
busy, distracted.

Okay then listen to me.

You tell me about the lady who stops by the store every
day, never buys anything, just stares at the row of
wooden horses. You tell me how you walked the extra
mile to get your favourite diner coffee, chortling eggs
and beans while watching the busker ignite one-half of a weary
skyline.

This way, you can tell your friends we still talk.

*There's more than one way
to get to the heart of things*

茶:

You tell me about driftwood, sangria, cherry blossoms
and tea, while splitting an orange down the middle,
spooning the seeds off of its insides. I fall asleep, cord
entwined around my finger, having heard all about your
day. You listen to the rise and fall of my breath as you stir
your cup of tea,

long over-steeped, almost bitter to taste,
still waiting to hear mine.

The Butterfly Lovers
Also the tragic love story of 梁山伯 and 祝英臺

There was once a butterfly caught on the headstone between 9th and 20th boulevard. The young man with a pea-blossom coat touched it and it became an ampersand from a poem. The ampersand untangled itself from a sea of letters and it became a savannah, warm but disquieting like the arms of a lover. The savannah hadn't seen the arms of a lover in many years and it became a turntable, shuffling between two equally indifferent songs like a moth and the flickering garden torch. The moth talks about the Am, how it's both morning on the Amtrak and A minor, the saddest chord in history. A minor is the child bent over the headstone, not knowing that, twenty years later, he would ever release the butterfly. There was once a butterfly caught on the headstone between 9th and 20th boulevard. But the butterfly was long dead, and the boulevard only a young man's memory.

The Weaver Girl and the Oxherd

梦河。Say 梦和。
Like, in our dreams,
we'll always be together.

But only, and if only.
In our dreams.

The Dream

The humming of the forest. The sparrows throwing the
wind into a tailspin. Against the midnight-green
backlight of the gas station, the tank half-full, I watched
the meter jump like a clock—the hand of time moving forward
with irredeemable certainty. From the next kiosk, the
man in a checkered shirt looks over, rubbing his tar-
stained hands across his jeans.

"Where are you headed?"

"Nowhere."

He chuckled, "I've been there once before." He turns his
cap over his head of silver. "It was glorious."

He chuckles again, slower this time, and climbs into his pickup
truck. "Be safe, kid," he smiles wryly. "Not many make it back."

My tank was full, car humming forest green. The sky
flushed pink, luminous as the ocean. I stepped on the
gas, the last ink of sunlight disappearing from my
bonnet. That's the beauty of Nowhere. The ghost of a life
and the way we'd drive on till morning.

ACKNOWLEDGMENTS

Thank you to my family, Dexter Chim, Celine Yeo and Chim Ler Ting, for their boundless enthusiasm and fervent support for my work.

Thank you to the following journals who have allowed me to grace their pages with the earlier versions of the following poems: "Beyond The Lake" in *A Velvet Giant*, 藕断丝连 in *The Normal School*, 追求梦想 in *Timber Journal*, "On The Black-and-White Television, Our Lies Look A Little Less White" and "Casual Chinese (n.)" in *Cherry Moon: Emerging Voices From The Asian Diaspora*, "Brane Theory" in *Colorado Review*, "That Language You're Trying to Learn When You are Sixty and Sitting at the Table with Your New-Found Friends Wondering when You Stopped Trying to Ask for Sauce" in *The Oxonian Review* and "Bak Kut Teh" in *Mascara Review*.

AUTHOR'S BIOGRAPHY

Chim Sher Ting is a Singaporean-Chinese writer. She is a 2021 Writeability Fellow with Writers Victoria and 2023 Kenyon Review Winter Workshop participant. She is a 2021-22 Pushcart and Best of The Net nominee with work published or forthcoming in *Prairie Schooner, Gulf Coast, Salt Hill, Colorado Review, Pleiades, AAWW's The Margins, OSU The Journal* and others. Her debut chapbook, *Bodies of Separation*, is published with Cathexis Northwest Press. She tweets at @sherttt and writes at sherting.com.

www.ingramcontent.com/pod-product-compliance
Lightning Source LLC
Chambersburg PA
CBHW051249120626
46547CB00014B/1858